12 WOMEN IN
EQUALITY AND
SOCIAL JUSTICE

by Brianna L. DeVore

12

STORY LIBRARY
MORE TO EXPLORE

www.12StoryLibrary.com

Copyright © 2020 by 12-Story Library, Mankato, MN 56002. All rights reserved. No part of this book may be reproduced or utilized in any form or by any means without written permission from the publisher.

12-Story Library is an imprint of Bookstaves.

Photographs ©: Derek Storm/Everett Collection/Alamy, cover, 1; Bonarov/CC4.0, 4; Rama/CC2.0, 5; Randall Studio/PD, 6; JT Vintage/Alamy, 7; Napoleon Sarony/PD, 8; Carl Deeg/PD, 9; Album/Alamy, 10; PD, 11; Jay Godwin/PD, 12; Richard Thornton/Shutterstock.com, 13; K. Kendall/CC2.0, 14; Robert Alexander/Getty Images, 15; Lynn Gilbert/CC4.0, 16; Supreme Court of the United States/PD, 17; Lynn Gilbert/CC4.0, 18; Rena Schild/Shutterstock.com, 19; Ms. magazine/CC4.0, 19; Green Belt Movement, 20; Green Belt Movement, 21; Berkeley Center for New Media/CC2.0, 22; Everett Collection Inc/Alamy, 23; Cinema Politica/CC2.0, 24; Sarah LittleRedfeather, 25; The Office of Congressman Ted Deutch/PD, 26; Mobilus In Mobili/CC2.0, 27; Fronteiras do Pensamento/CC2.0, 28; Kevin Andre Elliott/CC2.0, 29

ISBN
9781632357779 (hardcover)
9781632358868 (paperback)
9781645820574 (ebook)

Library of Congress Control Number: 2019938622

Printed in the United States of America
September 2019

About the Cover
Angela Davis in 2018.

Access free, up-to-date content on this topic plus a full digital version of this book. Scan the QR code on page 31 or use your school's login at 12StoryLibrary.com.

Table of Contents

Olympe de Gouges: Revolutionary Feminist

Olympe de Gouges was a French playwright and activist. She was born Marie Gouze in 1748. Her mother was a maid and her father was a butcher. Nuns taught her to read and write. Like many women at that time, she married young. She didn't like being a wife. She wanted to be a writer.

When she was 18, her husband died. She moved to Paris and changed her name to Olympe de Gouges. She started writing plays, novels, and political pamphlets. Many of her plays had strong political messages. But theaters would not accept her work because she was a woman. Her plays didn't make it to the stage until 1789. The first of her plays to be performed was about the cruelty of slavery.

An 18th century portrait of Olympe de Gouges.

In 1791, France was in the middle of a revolution. The people no longer wanted to be ruled by a king. They wanted to form their own government. Gouges wrote a political pamphlet called *The Declaration of the Rights of Woman and of the Female Citizen*. She demanded that this new government give women equal

The French Revolution began after the people of France stormed the Bastille, a royal prison in Paris.

rights. Her pamphlet is thought to be the first published document of the feminist movement.

41
Number of plays Olympe de Gouges wrote

- Only four of her plays were performed in her lifetime.
- Gouges believed all people should have equal rights.
- She was executed for her beliefs in 1793.

THE FRENCH REVOLUTION

On July 14, 1789, a royal prison in Paris was attacked by angry French citizens. This started the French Revolution. For years before, the French people dealt with starvation, joblessness, and high taxes. The fancy lifestyle of King Louis XVI and Queen Marie Antoinette angered them even more. Both king and queen were executed in 1793. The revolution ended in 1799.

Sojourner Truth: Speaking Out Against Slavery

Sojourner Truth in 1870.

I SELL THE SHADOW TO SUPPORT THE SUBSTANCE.
SOJOURNER TRUTH.

East Grand Circus Park,
DETROIT.

Randall

away from her parents. Her new slaveholder beat her. In 1810, Isabella was sold to the Dumont family. She spent 15 years with the Dumonts. During that time, she married and had five children. John Dumont promised to set her free in 1826. But when the time came, he changed his mind. Isabella was determined to be free. She decided to run away.

She believed God wanted her to travel and share her story. She

In the years leading up to the Civil War, Sojourner Truth traveled throughout the United States. She gave speeches about the evils of slavery. She spoke from experience.

She was born Isabella Baumfree in 1797. When she was nine years old, she was sold

THINK ABOUT IT

Because Sojourner Truth couldn't read or write, she told her story to a friend. The friend wrote it down. We can still read the *Narrative of Sojourner Truth* today. Why is this important?

would help others realize the cruelty of slavery. She changed her name to Sojourner Truth. "Sojourn" means to stay someplace for only a short time.

Sojourner Truth made many famous speeches. One is known as her "Ain't I A Woman?" speech. She delivered it in Akron, Ohio, in 1851. In it she described the discrimination she faced as a woman and as a black person. Truth often spoke about the rights of women. This angered some abolitionists who believed women's rights were not as important as ending slavery.

$100
Price a slaveholder paid in 1806 for Sojourner Truth and a flock of sheep

- The actual name of Truth's 1851 speech is "On Women's Rights."
- Twelve years after Truth gave the speech, a white woman changed it.
- Truth never learned to read or write.

Truth gives one of her passionate speeches.

Susan B. Anthony: Fighting for the Right to Vote

With her friend Elizabeth Cady Stanton, Susan B. Anthony made people aware of the women's suffrage movement. The two met in 1851. Back then, women could not own property, keep the money they earned, or work in many jobs. Anthony and Stanton knew this wouldn't change until women had the right to vote. Their friendship lasted over 50 years. Stanton wrote many of Anthony's speeches.

Anthony was born in 1820 in Adams, Massachusetts. Her father treated his sons and daughters equally. Anthony and her siblings were not given toys. They focused on chores and education. Anthony learned to read and write at three years old. At 19, she became a teacher. She taught for many years before returning to her family's farm in New York. The farm was a meeting place for the antislavery movement. These meetings inspired Anthony.

By 1856, Anthony was active in both the women's suffrage and antislavery movements. Some abolitionists wanted women to wait for voting rights until formerly enslaved

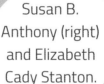

Susan B. Anthony (right) and Elizabeth Cady Stanton.

The signing of the 19th constitutional amendment in 1919, known as the "Anthony Amendment," giving women the right to vote.

black men had the right to vote. Anthony believed voting rights for both groups needed to happen at the same time.

Anthony voted in the 1872 presidential election. This was illegal. She hoped to gain voting rights through the courts. The judge decided against her before she entered the courtroom. Disappointed, she went back to fighting for a constitutional amendment. In 1878, a version of this amendment went to Congress. It wouldn't pass until 1919. In 1920, women in the United States were finally allowed to vote. Anthony had died 14 years earlier.

13,000
Number of miles (20,922 km) Susan B. Anthony traveled in 1871

- For decades, she went by train, carriage, horseback, boat, and sleigh to remote cities across the country.
- She often slept in railroad stations.
- Audiences harassed, booed, and insulted her for speaking about women's rights.

Simone de Beauvoir: Radical Ideas

A novelist, memoirist, and philosopher, Beauvoir had unique ideas. She is best known for her 1949 book *Le Deuxième Sexe*, or *The Second Sex*. This is one of the most important books in feminist thought.

Simone Lucie-Ernestine-Marie-Bertrand de Beauvoir was born in Paris in 1908. Her family was middle class. Her mother sent her to Catholic school. Her father encouraged her curiosity and love of learning.

In 1929, Beauvoir passed a difficult philosophy exam. Her score was the second best in the class. Another student named Jean-Paul Sartre had the top score. Beauvoir and Sartre became close friends and partners. They spent their days in French

Simone de Beauvoir in 1959.

THINK ABOUT IT

In 1953, *The Second Sex* was translated into English. The American publisher worried it wouldn't sell well. Fifteen percent of the text was removed. Some of Beauvoir's meanings were changed. Do you agree with these decisions? Why or why not?

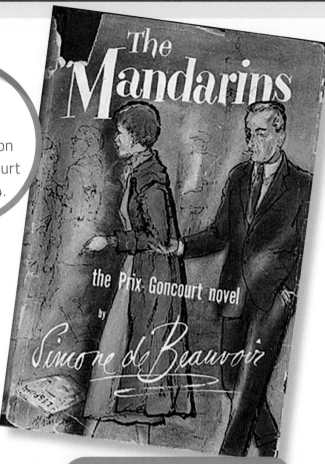

Beauvoir's book, *The Mandarins*, won France's Goncourt Prize in 1954.

cafés, writing and discussing ideas. Many other important thinkers of the time would join them.

Some of Beauvoir's work was shaped by war. She protested Germany's occupation of France during World War II. In 1962, she wrote a book about a woman's experience of violence during the Algerian War.

Her book *The Second Sex* describes how women are treated as objects while men are treated as people. Beauvoir used examples from history, religion, literature, and other subject areas to make her case. Her conclusion asks for equal treatment. It also describes a woman's need to freely create and express her individuality. These ideas were revolutionary and are still being discussed today.

7
Number of memoirs Simone de Beauvoir wrote

- Until the 2000s, Beauvoir was more popular in France for her memoirs and novels than for *The Second Sex*.
- She wrote her first novel, *She Came to Stay*, in 1943.
- She won France's Goncourt Prize for her 1954 novel *The Mandarins*.

Dolores Huerta: Helping Farmworkers Live Better Lives

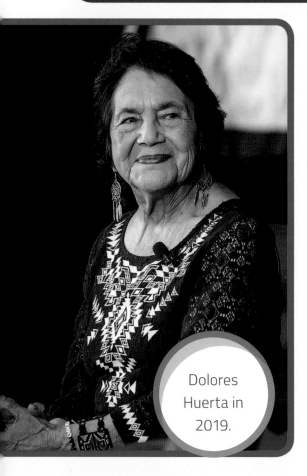

Dolores Huerta in 2019.

90 cents
Highest pay per hour a farmworker could earn before the UFW strike

- The workers were in the fields from sunup to sundown without water or toilets.
- Their homes had dirt floors. They used cardboard boxes as furniture.
- Women were vulnerable to abuse. Their children often worked alongside them.

She was born Dolores Fernandez in New Mexico in 1930. When she was three, her mother bought a hotel in California and gave free rooms to poor farmworkers. Huerta became a teacher after college. Her students were the children of farmworkers. They came to class hungry and barefoot. Huerta wanted to do more for these children. She would eventually have 11 children of her own.

Dolores Huerta was once accused of cheating on a school paper. Her teacher didn't think Hispanics could write that well. Experiences like this one influenced Huerta to work for change.

In 1962, Huerta and César Chávez founded the United Farm Workers (UFW). This was a union for grape farmworkers. Many were illegal immigrants. Some could not speak English. White growers took advantage of them. In 1965, Huerta helped organize a workers' strike. In 1975, a law giving California farmworkers the right to fight for better wages and conditions finally passed.

Huerta also led a national boycott of grapes. It stopped 17 million people from buying grapes. In 2012, she received the Presidential Medal of Freedom for her work.

RACE AND THE ENVIRONMENT

Pesticides are poisons used in fields to kill bugs. Thousands of grape workers suffered from cancer, birth defects, nosebleeds, and more because of these poisons. Many died. The UFW fought to ban them. Their efforts brought awareness to the fact that people of color are more likely to live and work around pollution than whites. This is called environmental racism. It is still a problem today.

The Dolores Huerta Foundation stages a march for immigrant farm workers' rights in 2017.

Audre Lorde: The Power of Words

Audre Lorde's use of language changed the way activists think. She was born in New York City in 1934. As a girl, she changed Audrey, her birth name, to Audre. She didn't like how the tail of the "y" hung down.

Lorde's parents were immigrants from the West Indies. Her mother spoke a mix of English and her native language. When her mother couldn't think of a word, she'd make one up. Blending real and imagined language inspired Lorde. Poetry helped her put emotions into words. When she couldn't find poems to express her emotions, she started to write her own.

Lorde got a master's degree in library science in 1961. She married and had two children. In 1986, her first book of poetry was published. That year, she went to Mississippi to teach writing. She discovered a love of teaching. She fell in love with a woman.

Between 1970 and 1978, Lorde published five more books of poetry. Her poems explored love, identity, sexuality, race, gender, and politics. Her 1980 book, *The Cancer Journals*, described her fight with breast cancer. She died of cancer in 1992.

Audre Lorde in 1980.

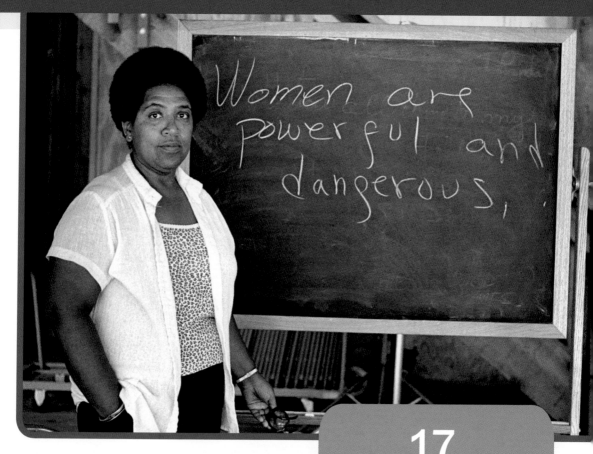

NOT ONE, BUT MANY

Lorde described herself as a "black, lesbian, mother, warrior, poet." She didn't value any one of these parts over the others. Both the civil rights movement and the feminist movement focused on one part of a person's identity. Lorde thought people should understand how all the parts interact with one another, or intersect. Today this is called intersectionality. It has changed the way a lot of activists think and work.

17
Audre Lorde's age when her first poem was published

- Lorde sold it to *Seventeen* magazine. She made more money from that sale than she earned for the next 10 years.
- It was a love poem. Her school's magazine rejected it for being inappropriate.
- She published many of her early poems under the pseudonym Rey Domini.

Ruth Bader Ginsburg: A Life in the Law

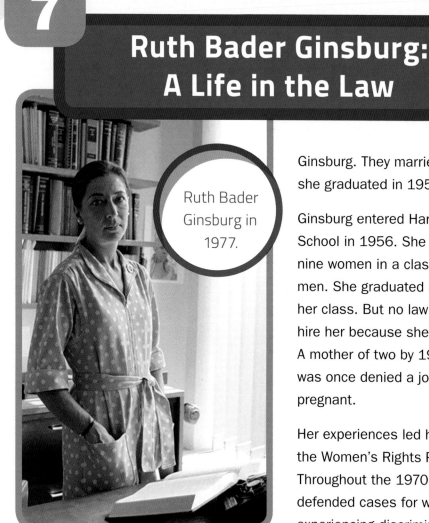

Ruth Bader Ginsburg in 1977.

Joan Ruth Bader was born in 1933 in New York City to a working-class family. Her father was a Jewish immigrant from Russia. She learned from her mother to value education, hard work, and independence. She went to Cornell University, where she met Marty

Ginsburg. They married shortly after she graduated in 1954.

Ginsburg entered Harvard Law School in 1956. She was one of nine women in a class of over 500 men. She graduated at the top of her class. But no law firm would hire her because she was a woman. A mother of two by 1965, she was once denied a job for being pregnant.

Her experiences led her to cofound the Women's Rights Project. Throughout the 1970s, Ginsburg defended cases for women experiencing discrimination. She argued that it was unconstitutional to deny equal rights to women. She won five of the six cases she argued before an all-male Supreme Court.

In 1993, Ginsburg became the second woman ever appointed to the Supreme Court. She has continued to support equal rights as a Supreme Court justice.

THE SUPREME COURT

The founders created the Supreme Court in the US Constitution. It is the highest level of the judicial branch of government. The court has one chief justice and eight associate justices. They usually serve for life. The president appoints a justice. That person must then be confirmed by Congress. The Supreme Court makes sure Congress and the president do not violate the Constitution. The Court also protects civil rights.

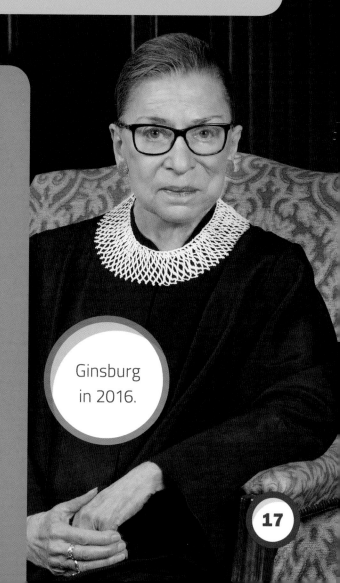

Ginsburg in 2016.

2013

Year when Ginsburg disagreed with the majority of the Supreme Court in *Shelby County v. Holder*

- This decision opened the door to race-based voter discrimination.
- People showed support for Ginsburg's argument by starting a movement. They called her "the Notorious RBG" on books, T-shirts, tattoos, and more.
- The nickname refers to rapper The Notorious B.I.G. Ginsburg has said the comparison is natural.

17

Gloria Steinem: Women's Movement Leader

Gloria Steinem was a spokesperson for the 1970s women's movement. She was born in 1934 in Toledo, Ohio. Her mother was a successful journalist who gave up her career to marry and raise a family. She suffered from mental illness. From childhood until college, Steinem took care of her mother.

Steinem's father was a traveling salesman. He took her, along with her mother and sister, on long road trips. Steinem did not attend school regularly. But she loved to learn. By seventh grade, she was reading a book a day.

After graduating college in 1956, Steinem spent two years in India. She learned nonviolent activism from followers of Mahatma Gandhi. In 1960, she moved to New York City. She wanted to be a political journalist. Her bosses wanted her to write about beauty, fashion, and housework. Steinem knew this was because she was a woman. She realized her mother had faced the same obstacles.

Steinem wanted to write about issues facing women. In 1971, she cofounded *Ms.* magazine. It covered

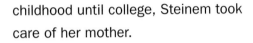

Gloria Steinem in 1977.

Steinem receiving the Presidential Medal of Freedom from President Obama in 2013.

feminist topics such as equal pay for women and domestic violence. Steinem traveled the country to speak on these issues.

Because Steinem was beautiful, many news programs wanted to interview her. She was often asked why she wasn't married. She wanted to be known for her work, not for her looks. She was determined not to let sexism get the best of her. Steinem became known for her calm presence and intelligence.

2,000
Number of female delegates who attended the 1977 National Women's Conference

- The conference was held in Houston, Texas. Steinem rates organizing it as one of her greatest accomplishments.
- Women from every state attended.
- Runners carried a torch from Seneca Falls, New York, to Houston. Seneca Falls was the site of the first women's rights convention in 1848.

9

Wangari Maathai: Saving the Environment

Wangari Maathai.

51 million+

Number of trees the Green Belt Movement planted in Kenya's mountainous regions

- The movement is led mostly by women.
- Along with planting trees, the women work to promote democracy, create gender equality, and fight climate change.
- The movement is now international. Tree-planting efforts have begun in several other countries.

As a child, Wangari Maathai played in the streams and forest near her home. A giant fig tree stood close by. Her mother said it was a tree of God. Respect for nature was part of Maathai's culture. It guided her for the rest of her life.

She was born in 1940 and grew up in Nakuru, Kenya. Her father was a mechanic for a white settler. Kenya was a British colony then. Maathai's parents encouraged her to go to school. She got a scholarship to Mount St. Scholastica College in Kansas and earned a Bachelor of Science degree. In time, she became the first East African woman to earn a PhD.

Maathai returned to Kenya in 1966. It was now an independent country. But the trees and streams from her youth were gone. Kenya's government had continued the deforestation begun by the British. Women did not have enough firewood for cooking. Children were starving.

In 1977, Maathai started the Green Belt Movement. She taught women how to plant native trees. She led protests to fight the government's efforts to destroy natural land. In 2004, she became the first African woman to win the Nobel Peace Prize.

COLONIAL AFRICA

Kenya was a British colony because of something called the Berlin Conference. In 1884, leaders from 14 European countries and the United States got together in Germany. They wanted to take Africa's natural resources to make their own countries richer. They drew boundaries on an African map. These became countries. Then they took control of these areas. No Africans were involved.

A Green Belt Movement tree nursery in Kenya.

Angela Davis: Fighting Injustice

Angela
Davis
in 2018.

By 1967, Davis was teaching at the University of California, San Diego. She was a member of the Communist Party. She also worked for the Black Panther Party. The Panthers believed in black dignity and in protecting black people from police brutality. Davis received death threats daily for her work with these groups. She bought guns to protect herself.

On August 7, 1970, one of her friends took the guns. He and three others ended up dead. Because the guns belonged to Davis, she was charged with murder. She went into hiding but was eventually arrested.

Under chants of "Free Angela," a worldwide movement rose up to support her. John Lennon and Yoko Ono wrote a song about her. She was found not guilty in 1972. Since

Angela Davis has been a teacher, activist, and political prisoner. She has always fought for her beliefs. She was born in Birmingham, Alabama, in 1944. Both her parents were teachers. In 1965, she graduated from Brandeis University. She quickly became known for her intelligence.

Davis at a rally in 1974.

then, Davis has focused on fighting racism, freeing political prisoners, and protesting corporate prisons.

CORPORATE PRISONS

In the 1970s and '80s, laws were passed that gave longer sentences for drug charges. Government prisons could not handle all the new inmates this created. Corporations started building and running private prisons. Corporate prisons are run for profit. Many people think corporate prisons are a bad idea.

40

Percent of US prisoners who are African American, as of 2018

- The United States imprisons more people than any other country in the world.
- Prisoners working in corporate prisons make 20 to 31 cents per hour.
- Many activists consider this to be modern-day slavery.

Winona LaDuke: Protecting the Earth

Winona LaDuke in 2018.

While studying at Harvard in 1977, LaDuke learned about the American Indian Movement (AIM). The work of these Native American activists inspired her. At 18, she addressed the United Nations on the rights of Native Americans. After graduating, she moved to the White Earth Reservation in northern Minnesota. These were the lands of her father's people.

Winona LaDuke believes in a return to indigenous ways of life. She was born in California in 1959. In Ojibwe, her name means "first-born daughter." Ojibwe is the language of the Anishinaabe people. LaDuke's mother was a Jewish artist, and her father was an Ojibwe activist.

Over 90 percent of the tribe's land was lost in treaties. LaDuke founded the White Earth Land Recovery Project in 1989 to get some of this land back. By 1996, the project had bought back 1,000 acres (404.7 hectares). It also focused on planting native foods and creating renewable energy sources, like solar panels. LaDuke's work gained attention from presidential candidate Ralph Nader. In both 1996 and 2000, she ran as his vice president.

200

Miles (322 km) Winona LaDuke traveled on horseback for her 2018 "Love Water Not Oil" ride

- The ride followed a proposed pipeline route.
- Some Ojibwe people believe oil is part of an Ojibwe myth. The myth warns of a black snake that rises from the ground to cause destruction.
- The myth says that people must rise against this snake. If they don't, the world will end.

In 2013, LaDuke put her land recovery project on hold. An oil company planned to run a pipeline through Ojibwe land. The pipeline would threaten lakes full of wild rice. The rice is sacred to the Ojibwe people. LaDuke is devoted to protesting pipelines.

LaDuke on her "Love Water Not Oil" ride in 2018.

Emma González: Ending Gun Violence

Emma González is a voice for better gun control. She was born in 1999 and grew up in Parkland, Florida. Her father is a Cuban immigrant. A natural leader, González headed her high school's gay-straight alliance (GSA) for three years.

González was at school on February 14, 2018, when a former student entered the building and started shooting. He killed 17 people and injured 17 others. González's friend Carmen was one of the people killed.

Three days later, González spoke at a gun control rally. She challenged politicians to change gun laws. She called on students to stand up against gun violence. Video of her speech went viral. News programs invited her on for interviews.

Time magazine put her on their cover.

González teamed up with other survivors from that day. They started March for Our Lives. This nonprofit educates people on gun laws and voting. Each state has different gun laws. Some states do very little to control who can buy a gun. Stricter

Emma González in 2018.

González leads a moment of slience at the March for Our Lives Rally in Washington, DC, in 2018.

gun laws in Florida might have prevented the shooting.

March for Our Lives grew quickly. A year after the tragedy, there were more than 200 chapters throughout the United States. Their efforts helped pass 67 gun control or gun violence prevention laws in the US in 2018.

THINK ABOUT IT

González proved that young peoples' voices matter. What issue are you passionate about? What can you do to make a difference?

1 million+

Protestors who took part in March for Our Lives rallies on March 24, 2018

- More than 800 rallies occurred in 38 different countries.
- Washington, DC, had the largest turnout, with over 200,000 people.
- González led a moment of silence at the DC rally. It lasted 6 minutes and 20 seconds, the same amount of time the Parkland shooter was active.

Out of the Shadows

Gloria Anzaldúa

Gloria Anzaldúa was a queer Chicana poet and feminist. She wrote in a mix of English and Spanish. This reflected the discomfort of being multicultural in the US. She believed building friendships between white women and women of color could help battle their shared oppression.

Leymah Gbowee

In 2003, Leymah Gbowee led a protest of the 14-year civil war in Liberia. The mix of Muslim and Christian women barricaded peace talks with their bodies. They would not let leaders leave until they came to an agreement. She won a Nobel Peace Prize for these efforts.

Leymah Gbowee in 2013.

Barbara Smith

In the 1970s, Barbara Smith worked with other black lesbian feminists to create the Combahee River Collective Statement. This defined black feminism. Both a movement and a field of academic study, black feminism is Smith's lifelong passion. She also cofounded the Kitchen Table Press in 1980 with Audre Lorde.

Barbara Smith.

Pauline Tangiora

Pauline Tangiora is a tribal elder of the Māori, an indigenous tribe in northern New Zealand. She has fought for the rights of indigenous peoples for over 40 years. In 2016, she won a long legal battle. She received money for damages caused by colonizers.

Glossary

abolitionist
Someone who wants to end slavery.

activist
Someone who takes action for social or political change.

amendment
A change to a legal document.

colony
A place taken by another country.

deforestation
Removing large amounts of trees from a forest.

feminism
Belief in the equal rights of women and men.

indigenous
Original occupants.

philosopher
A person who wants to understand life.

pseudonym
A made-up name a writer uses instead of their real name.

sexism
Treating people unfairly because of their sex. This happens most often to women.

strike
Refusing to work because of poor treatment.

suffrage
The right to vote.

treaties
Agreements between two independent nations.

union
An organization of workers that protects their rights.

Read More

Carmon, Irin, and Shana Knizhnik. *Notorious RBG Young Readers' Edition: The Life and Times of Ruth Bader Ginsburg*. New York: HarperCollins, 2017.

Grimes, Nikki. *Chasing Freedom: The Life Journeys of Harriet Tubman and Susan B. Anthony, Inspired by Historical Facts*. New York: Scholastic, 2015.

Paul, Caroline. *You Are Mighty: A Guide to Changing the World*. New York: Bloomsbury Publishing, 2018.

Swanson, Jennifer. *Environmental Activist Wangari Maathai*. STEM Trailblazer Biographies. Minneapolis, MN: Lerner Publishing Group, 2018.

Weatherford, Carole Boston. *Voice of Freedom: Fannie Lou Hamer: The Spirit of the Civil Rights Movement*. Somerville, MA: Candlewick Press, 2015.

Visit 12StoryLibrary.com

Scan the code or use your school's login at **12StoryLibrary.com** for recent updates about this topic and a full digital version of this book. Enjoy free access to:

- Digital ebook
- Breaking news updates
- Live content feeds
- Videos, interactive maps, and graphics
- Additional web resources

Note to educators: Visit 12StoryLibrary.com/register to sign up for free premium website access. Enjoy live content plus a full digital version of every 12-Story Library book you own for every student at your school.

Index

About the Author

Brianna L. DeVore has a bachelor's degree in women's studies and works in the publishing industry. She lives in Minnesota with her husband, cat, and two dogs.

READ MORE FROM 12-STORY LIBRARY

Every 12-Story Library Book is available in many fomats. For more information, visit **12StoryLibrary.com**